T0277213

WAGONS IN THE PEAK DISTRICT

PAUL HARRISON

AMBERLEY

Acknowledgements

Thanks must go to Peter Butterworth and Frank Emerson of Tarmac Buxton Lime & Cement for granting permission to use the photographs of the wagons from my visit to Tunstead in April 2008 and the new cement tanks seen in July 2003. I would also like to thank Mike Fraser for the 'gen' on the BLI JGA and Lafarge JPA cement tanks at the time they were delivered new. Finally, to my fellow wagon enthusiasts, and in particular Tom Smith for giving me inspiration to write further books after being given the chance to help with the publication of his trio of books on modern wagons more than ten years ago.

First published 2023

Amberley Publishing
The Hill, Stroud
Gloucestershire, GL5 4EP

www.amberley-books.com

Copyright © Paul Harrison, 2023

The right of Paul Harrison to be identified as the Author of this work has been asserted in accordance with the Copyrights, Designs and Patents Act 1988.

ISBN 978 1 3981 0874 5 (print)
ISBN 978 1 3981 0875 2 (ebook)

British Library Cataloguing in Publication Data.
A catalogue record for this book is available from the British Library.

Typesetting by SJmagic DESIGN SERVICES, India.
Printed in the UK.

Introduction

In my first book for Amberley Publishing, *Freight in the Peak District*, I looked at the different railfreight traffic flows that have operated in the Peak District area of England between 2000 and 2018 using my own photographs and notes to describe and illustrate the different trains. The railfreight scene is constantly changing as flows start and end, and different railfreight operators move the large tonnages of raw limestone, aggregates, and cement from the Peak District area to terminals all over mainland UK. And so, the timetables that these trains follow change a lot too, often by the day or week and many paths are what are termed conditional. This means, for example, that of three paths departing, say, from Dowlow to three different terminals, only one of these will depart on a particular day of the week. The other two paths remain unused until the customer at the second terminal requires a delivery and the flow switches to serve that one instead, and hopefully by the end of the week all three terminals have been served from Dowlow. As I finished writing this introduction in September 2021, the country is very much still in the uncertain times that have changed many aspects of life and work due to the Covid-19 pandemic. Railfreight in the UK had to adapt very quickly to these changes and essential freight flows were prioritised and non-essential flows stopped or reduced to suit. The construction industry therefore had a rapid reduction in the quantity of raw material being transported across the country as a result.

The four rail-connected quarries in the Peak District are Dove Holes, Tunstead, Hindlow and Dowlow. When I originally started to write this introduction in 2020, all quarries except Hindlow sent out large tonnages of limestone and graded aggregates. Up until mid-2020, Hindlow was still only receiving trainloads of limestone from Tunstead on an as required basis, although two return paths per day were available. However, as of September 2020, Hindlow stopped receiving limestone from Tunstead, and instead there was a resumption of quarrying. A mobile crusher and screening system is used to produce different grades of limestone on-site. A thousand tonnes of this limestone is used by the existing Maerz limekilns. These kilns are used to produce a range of trademark named lime products. The remaining crushed stone is destined for the High Speed 2 railway project, construction of which is well underway in the Home Counties and Midlands.

So, it just goes to show that not everything stays the same. Dove Holes quarry is now owned and operated by Cemex; Tunstead and Hindlow quarries are now part of Tarmac Buxton Lime & Cement (a CRH company); Dowlow is now owned by the Breedon Group. The two rail-connected cement works are Hope, owned by the Breedon Group, and Tunstead again owned by Tarmac Buxton Lime & Cement.

The Buxton Sidings Extension Scheme to upgrade and lengthen the run-round known as the Up Relief siding (URS) was completed in spring 2019 and officially opened on 29 April 2019. The £14 million project allows longer trains of loaded and empty wagons to operate from and to Hindlow and Dowlow. The scheme allows up to two trains to use the new URS run-round loops. However, my own daytime observations have only noted single trains of up to twenty-four wagons using the URS loops. The original URS loop had a maximum train length of 505 metres, which equated to a capacity of around 1,750 tonnes, or eighteen wagons. By extending the existing sidings northwards by approximately 422 metres (from the existing buffer stop to the proposed buffer stop), this created the necessary infrastructure to allow an increase in freight train capacity to a train length of 505 m, with a capacity of around 2,600 tonnes or twenty-six wagons. A cross-over is provided roughly in line with the original loop turnout, and a single turnout and head-shunt is located at the northern end of the extension.

The existing public footpath that crosses over the Stockport to Buxton railway line was extended by adding a new footbridge up and over the new URS lines. This footbridge makes a pretty good vantage point for trains coming and going from the Hindlow branch, which is the remaining section of the Buxton to Ashbourne line. Although Buxton Up Relief sidings is the official railway name, they are locally known as 'Donarue' or 'Donnahue sidings' depending on which version you know or who you ask.

There have been calls to reopen the former Midland Railway main line through the Peak District to help supply materials for the HS2 project and provide future network capacity. This idea would have the benefit of avoiding the steeply graded section through Peak Forest and also reduce the amount of freight on the existing Hope Valley route. Stone traffic would be routed towards Derby via Matlock instead, then onward to their eventual destinations in the Midlands, East Anglia, and Home Counties. This would be a long-term project that would involve reacquisition of land, structures, and rights of way. There is also the issue of moving the cycle and walkways, plus the Peak Rail heritage railway that occupies the original line formation between Rowsley and Matlock.

Traffic from the area is conveyed in a variety of bogie air-braked hoppers, open box, and tank wagons and most are now owned by wagon leasing companies or the railfreight operators. However, this was not always the case and as the photographs will illustrate there has been a shift away from the quarry and cement companies owning and operating their own fleets of wagons in the past ten years or so. There has also been a move away from the traditional two-axle wagon designs that were built between the 1960s and 1990s for private owners. Modern bogie wagon designs offer a better tare weight to payload ratio and use 'track-friendly' suspension and bogies.

I have listed the photos in chronological date order to keep in theme with the Freight photographs seen in my first book for Amberley Publishing. I have gone further back in time to the year 1994 to better illustrate some of the wagons that were then used from Dove Holes and Tunstead quarries. I have included wagons that were commonly used from the main quarries and cement works along with others that only worked there for a short time, usually on a specific railfreight flow.

In the photo captions I list the wagon type, number, location, and date. I also explain the type of the work it was used for, the relevant livery and ownership details at that time. Given the nature of contracts and lifespan of the wagons illustrated, some appear more than once – especially if used from more than one quarry. Some wagons have received new branding or liveries, while others have had the original branding removed where appropriate. I wouldn't claim to have ever seen every type of wagon that has worked from the Peak District, but I have tried to illustrate the main ones, plus those that have simply visited or passed through. Peak Forest Up Holding sidings, for example, has seen many different designs of wagon pass through – some only for a day or so. Others like the long-time stored ZFV 'Dogfish' ballast wagon stayed for around fifteen years before removal in early 2014. The ever-changing railfreight market has meant that new wagons appear on some contracts and older wagons were repurposed elsewhere, especially those owned by wagon-leasing companies like Touax, VTG and Nacco. The now privatised freight operating companies have not held back either and over the past twenty years or so have introduced many new or converted wagon for the aggregates markets.

The photographs are all taken by me mainly around Peak Forest and the main quarry and cement works as appropriate. I have included photographs of the wagons in the local area like

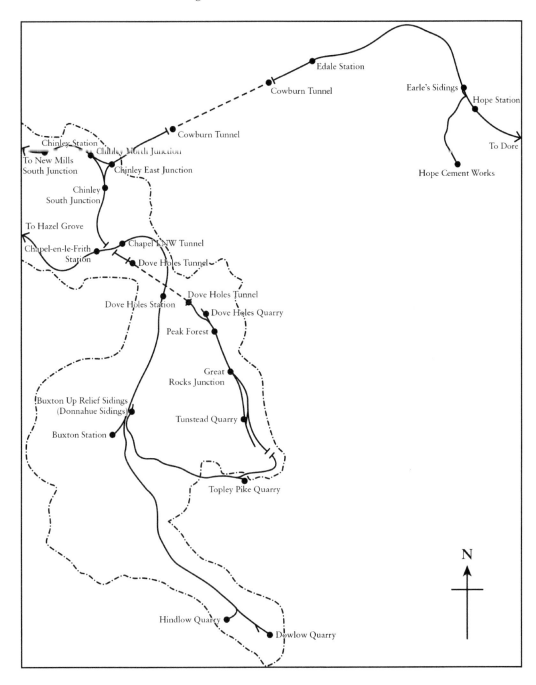

Cheshire and Derbyshire where these are known to work from the Peak District, working from or to one of the stone or cement works.

I have included another copy of the map published in my first book to help illustrate the different locations I have been able to view the wagons. To recap, the Peak District lies at the southern end of the Pennine Hills in northern England and in this sense encompasses the whole area as opposed to the actual Peak District National Park. Most of the main four quarries around Buxton are excluded and lie outside the park boundaries. Hope Cement works is however located inside the park (as is the former Topley Pike quarry). White Peak refers to the limestone areas of the park and Dark Peak the gritstone and other non-limestone areas. Also, Peak Forest is the railway name for the location, the actual place being Peak Dale, while the real Peak Forest village is just over 2 miles away to the east.

Thanks to go my partner Claire, my parents and family for their encouragement. I hope that you enjoy the photographic content in the book. I have enjoyed looking back through my collection, selecting photos to include and finding the information from my notes, books, and magazines.

Paul Harrison
Northwich

Postscript

Since writing this introduction in September 2021, a new quarry railhead will be commissioned shortly to enable stone to be loaded at Hillhead Quarry for HS2 construction traffic. The Tarmac-owned quarry has in effect been re-connected to the railway network again after the original connection was removed in the 1980s.

Bibliography

Brown, Joe, *Liverpool & Manchester Railway Atlas* (Manchester: Crecy Publishing Limited, 2021)

Dickenson, John and Chris, *Private Owner Wagon Fleet* (Bishop's Waltham & Southampton: South Coast Transport Publishing, 1990)

EMAP/Bauer Media, *RAIL – Wagons Roll (Wallace, Bob)/Wagons/Wagons News pages/ columns* – Issue 182 September 1992 to Issue 328 April 1998

Foursight Publications/Morton's Media Group, *Rail Express – Wallace's Wonderful World of Wagons (Wallace, Bob)/Wagons (Volland, Rob)/Wagons (Bayer, Gareth)* – Issue 1, June 1996 to present

Ifold, Peter and Mott, Stewart, *Air Braked Series Wagon Fleet (Nos 100000 – 990049) Second Edition* (Hampshire: South Coast Transport Publishing, 1994)

Ifold, Peter and Mott, Stewart, *British Rail Wagon Fleet, Volume 5* (Portishead & Southampton: South Coast Transport Publishing, 1989)

Inter-City Railway Society, *ICRS Combined Wagon Sighting File/Datafile – Winter 2005 – Sixth Edition* (Birmingham: ICRS, 2006)

Inter-City Railway Society, *ICRS UK Rail Series No.3 – UK Combine Vol.2 2021 – 2nd Edition* (Birmingham: ICRS, 2021)

Marshall, Andrew, *Private Owner Wagons (Volume 1)* (Shipley: Metro Enterprises Ltd, 1989)

Marshall, Andrew, *Private Owner Wagons (Volume 1) Second Edition* (Shipley: Metro Enterprises Ltd, 1992)

Marshall, Andrew, *Private Owner Wagons (Volume 2)* (Shipley: Metro Enterprises Ltd, 1990)

KPA – 83 70 BR 690 5 008-1 – Peak Forest Reception sidings – 12 September 1994
Tiphook Rail-owned KPA 90 tonne glw bogie aggregate hoppers were used from Dove Holes quarry to supplement the existing RMC bogie hopper fleet. The wagon is in a much weathered white and blue livery with the prominent TR Tiphook Rail logo. A batch of twenty-five modified wagons were also used from Tunstead. A few years later, 104 KPAs became JJA auto-ballaster wagons. By 1996 thirty-six had been scrapped due to accidents or to provide spares.

JHA – PDUF 17951 – Peak Forest Reception sidings – January 1997
This unusual looking bogie hopper wagon was a prototype 102 t glw design constructed with an aluminium body and built by Powell Duffryn-Standard in 1993. It was built shortly before the Maindy wagon works in Cardiff closed. The wagon was intended to be first in a fleet of similar new wagons. The JHA wagon was used with the RMC JGA hoppers on workings from Dove Holes. It was later stored and scrapped at Marcroft Engineering, Stoke-on-Trent.

KPA – Peak Forest – January 1997

On a cold January afternoon in 1997, a brief visit to Peak Forest was rewarded with sight of the Tunstead to Ratcliffe power station loaded train passing under the Batham Gate Road overbridge. This is a very convenient vantage point for enthusiasts but the passing road traffic is a lot busier these days. This is one of the converted KPAs with the curved top end removed due to it being found to foul on part of the main loader at Tunstead when first tried in 1993.

KPAs – 33 70 6905 115-5 and 109-8 – Peak Forest Long sidings – 7 June 1998

By 1996, the Tiphook Rail KPA wagons were rather worn after several years constant usage in traffic. Wagons were initially overhauled for Tunstead traffic, the curved ends were removed and replaced with a straight end instead. This pair of blue KPAs are seen in Buxton Rail traffic stabled in the Long Siding. Fifteen KPAs were hired by Buxton Rail, a joint venture between RMC and BLI to supply stone to construct a new second runway at Manchester Airport.

PXA (KEA) – PR 3195 – Peak Forest Up Holding sidings – 7 June 1998
A rake of ten Procor-owned PXA bogie box wagons were parked up at Peak Forest during summer 1998, although I wasn't able to determine what traffic they were intended for. Later enquiries suggested they might have been used from Dove Holes to Leeds Balm Road stone terminal. No. PR 3195 was one of a batch of seventy-eight wagons originally built for Channel Tunnel construction traffic by Procor during 1987/8 at their Wakefield works.

JGA – RMC 17219 – Peak Forest – 27 February 2001
Until 1986 RMC operated a fleet of inherited ex-Peakstone PGA hoppers and hired in BR two-axle hoppers and tippler/box wagons for their traffic flows. The purchase of twenty-four new 90 t glw bogie hoppers from Standard Wagon Co. in 1986 enabled greater payloads to be transported from Dove Holes. The older BR vacuum-braked wagons were soon phased out. This wagon was overhauled by Wabtec, Doncaster, and painted in the revised RMC livery.

JIA – 33 70 9382 026-0 – Peak Forest Up Holding sidings – 27 February 2001
JIA 'Polybulk' bogie covered hopper wagons were used on the flow of powdered lime from the quarry at Dowlow to the PD Stirling distribution depot at Mossend. The lime was used in the manufacture of glass and the flow of traffic first started in the 1980s using different wagons. The JIA wagons were hired in from CAIB and worked alongside the PBA (later JAA) covered hoppers. The JIA wagons carried several versions of owner branding at different times.

CSAs – 876063 and 876060 – Peak Forest Up Holding sidings – 27 February 2001
A surprising addition to the EWS wagon fleet, back in 2000, was a small fleet of eight second-hand Rugby Cement PCA powder tankers. RFS Industries overhauled them to become CSA tank wagons. The wagons were used on a new to rail flow of quicklime from the then Buxton Lime Industries Hindlow quarry to Fifoots Point (aka Uskmouth B) power station near Newport in South Wales. Here a quartet of CSAs is seen at Peak Forest having just arrived from Hindlow.

MBA – 500043 – Peak Forest Reception sidings – 30 May 2001
In July 1999, EWS announced a deal with Thrall Europa that would see 2,500 new wagons built over a five-year period. In May 1999, the first of the new 102 t glw MBA bogie box wagons were being completed at York works. An access door was provided on each side of the wagon to enable the wagons to be cleaned inside when necessary. Seen here in traffic from Dove Holes, but they have been used from Tunstead and Dowlow too.

VKA – 210509 – Peak Forest – 30 May 2001
Railway vans were used to move bagged cement products from Hope works by rail in the years gone by. Investment at Hope enabled larger capacity vans to be loaded for despatch to new or reactivated terminals. Carlisle Brunthill in Cumbria and Moorswater in Cornwall were the main two. Here a pair of VKA vans (VGA vans fitted with modified axle journals) depart Peak Forest for Hope Earle's sidings tagged on the rear of a rake of seventeen PCA tanks.

MEAs – 391010 and 391390 – Peak Forest Up Holding sidings – 30 May 2001
This pair of MEAs were parked in an unusually empty Up Holding sidings. The idea of using recycled wagon chassis is often a low-cost solution to providing 'new' wagons. BR Railfreight Coal introduced a batch of forty-five converted MEAs for coal traffic in South Wales in 1990. Nos 391010 and 391390, dating from 1990 and 1997, are both conversions from surplus HEA coal wagons for Dowlow and Dove Holes aggregates traffic. Both are now scrapped.

ZZA – ADB965208 – Peak Forest Up Holding sidings – 30 May 2001
The traction depot at Buxton was home to a pair of independent snow ploughs. The Derbyshire High Peak area was often subject to extreme snowfall in the winter months and the snowploughs were essential to keep help the railway lines open. When Buxton TMD closed in 1997, the ploughs were transferred to Peak Forest initially. They were then refurbished and returned back to Peak Forest ready for action. No ploughs are now stabled at Peak Forest anymore.

JEA – BM 19706 – Peak Forest – 30 May 2001

The W.H. Davis-built 102 t JEA bogie limestone hoppers were ordered by Brunner Mond & Co. to replace the hired in CAIB PGA two-axle hoppers on the Tunstead to Northwich traffic. These PGAs had replaced the famous 47 t JGV vacuum-braked hoppers. The JGVs dated from the 1930s, 1940s and 1950s and had done sterling service for I.C.I. Mond and later Buxton Lime Industries. One JEA wagon effectively replaced two of the JGVs and looked smart with the BM logo.

YGB – DB 982780 'Seacow' – Peak Forest – 10 June 2001

Like most locations on the UK railway network, the infrastructure requires maintenance and civil engineering work from time to time. And this often means supplying fresh trainloads of railway ballast – often crushed granite to help bed the track into place and stop any movement. Here a rake of loaded 'Seacow' ballast hoppers are stabled in the Down & Up Through siding one Sunday at Peak Forest. Livery is faded, unbranded Transrail grey with red top band.

YGB – DB 980020 'Seacow' – Peak Forest – 10 June 2001
By contrast this 1981 BREL Shildon-built 'Seacow' looks in an even worse condition than the previous wagon. Rusted engineer's grey with yellow band would seem an apt livery description. The wagon has received a Mainline Freight branding sticker on the solebar. This design of ballast wagon has been replaced by new higher-capacity wagons, and at the time of writing only thirty-five YGA/YGBs were recorded as extant. All others were scrapped and some preserved.

JGA – BLI 19200 – Great Rocks – 10 June 2001
The doyen of the BLI fleet of JGA hopper wagons is seen parked at Great Rocks on the Up line, while the train engine Class 60 ran round the wagons. A batch of twenty JGAs were built in 1994 by Tatrastroj Poprad of Slovakia for new and existing limestone traffic from Tunstead to power stations including Ratcliffe and also to Hindlow. Limestone was moved the short distance to Hindlow by rail as at the time there was no limestone extraction on site at the time.

JIA – 33 70 9382 045-0 – Peak Forest Up Holding sidings – 23 October 2001
The powdered lime to Mossend traffic was at the time of this photograph sent via the EWS 'Enterprise' wagonload services, initially from Dowlow to Peak Forest then to Warrington Arpley. From there, loaded wagons were sent via a trunk working direct to Mossend Yard. A short shunt move later, they arrived at the PD Stirling railfreight terminal where the wagons were unloaded. Branded 'Traffic Services Polybulk' with a smaller sized CAIB logo.

CSAs – Peak Forest Up Holding sidings – 23 October 2001
The eight CSA tanks usually worked three or four wagons at a time. They were routed via the EWS 'Enterprise' trainload freight network. AES, who then owned Fifoots Point, had invested in the power station, which reopened in 2001. However, by 2002 AES had passed into receivership. The CSAs had a short operating life and apart from a brief trial in Dowlow lime traffic to PD Stirling, remained in store. All wagons except No. 876061 are now scrapped.

PCA – BCC 11032 – Peak Forest Reception sidings – 23 October 2001
A rake of cement tank wagons parked at Peak Forest may seem unusual at first. However, back in 2001, EWS still held the haulage contract for Blue Circle Cement. PCA tanks were used from Hope to Carlisle Brunthill depot along with VGA or VKA two-axle vans to carry palletised loads of bagged cement products. Occasionally, the IWB bogie vans were used too. The BCC two-axle and bogie cement wagons were once a common sight across the UK.

PCA – BCC 11101 – Peak Forest Reception sidings – 23 October 2001
This wagon and the one on the right have recently been overhauled and freshly painted in the plain grey livery used on the Blue Circle owned PCA fleet. Nos 11101 and 11064 were overhauled at the RFS (Engineering) works at Doncaster. At the time Blue Circle only operated the 'Metalair' straight barrelled tank version of the PCA from Hope. Virtually all of their 'Centre-depressed' or 'Vee-tanks' type PCA wagons were in store at the time.

TTA – BRT 57214 – Peak Forest Reception sidings – 23 October 2001
Gas oil traffic to fuel diesel-powered locomotives was once a large part of the railfreight scene. Most depots or stabling facilities like Buxton and later Peak Forest relied on regular deliveries of gas fuel oil to keep the wheels turning. Deliveries to Peak Forest usually arrived twice a week via the EWS 'Enterprise' trip feeder from Warrington Arpley. Here a former BRT-owned 46 t TTA tank has recently arrived and is parked in the reception sidings.

TUA – PR 70063 – Peak Forest Reception sidings – 23 October 2001
Also, at Peak Forest in the same rake as the TTA was this TUA 51 t diesel tank wagon in gas oil traffic. Built by Charles Roberts at Horbury works in 1973 for Procor. Forty-five tanks were built in this batch and were split into two fleets, one used by VIP Oils (twenty-five) and the other Carless Solvents Limited (twenty tanks). No. PR 70063 is still wearing the Carless and Procor branding, although both are long since gone, having been taken over and absorbed by other companies.

MEA – 391270 – Peak Forest Up Holding sidings – 22 November 2001
This wagon is from a batch of 100 converted for EWS by Marcroft Engineering in 1996/7. These were first to receive the EWS maroon and gold livery that replaced the MEA previous liveries. Other conversions from HEA domestic coal wagons include three SJA scrap carriers, and those recoded as RNA nuclear flask barrier wagons either with the hopper body intact or removed entirely and ballast weights added to the chassis. Used from Dowlow and Tunstead.

MEA – 391217 – Peak Forest Up Holding sidings – 22 November 2001
Prior to the formation of EWS, only Loadhaul and Mainline Freight ordered batches of MEA wagons intended for several different commodities. In time all of the MEAs became the property of EWS including the original Railfreight Coal examples. For a time, block trainloads using MEAs were rather colourful. This wagon was one of a batch of forty wagons converted by RFS at Doncaster in 1996 for Loadhaul painted in a black with white top capping livery.

IWB – 33 80 279 7 707-7 – Peak Forest Up Holding sidings – 22 November 2001
A pool of IWB Cargowaggon Habfis bogie vans were also used for bagged cement products traffic from Hope to Carlisle and Moorswater. Seven of these IWB vans were repainted into a Blue Circle yellow livery by RFS (E) with company lettering and the famous circle logo. Like the VKAs, the IWB vans turned up at Peak Forest like this one, in transit to or from Hope Earle's sidings, which by then was operated by rival Freightliner Heavy Haul.

TUA – PR 70117 – Peak Forest Up Holding sidings – 22 November 2001
Another TUA design of fuel oil tank, to a slightly different design to the previous TUA. No. PR 70017 was the last of a batch of twenty such tanks built by Norbrit-Pickering of Wishaw, near Motherwell, in 1974 for lessor Procor. These tanks were also rated at 51 t glw. Originally used by three different petroleum companies but later in a general user gas oil pool of similar TTA and TUA tanks owned by lessor CAIB. This wagon was last recorded as being stored.

HMA – 354947 – Peak Forest Up Holding sidings – 23 February 2002
During the period 2001 to 2008, it was possible to see merry-go-round (MGR) coal wagons at Peak Forest. They were usually defective wagons from Hope works or Earle's sidings. The wagons would be tripped Peak Forest initially and then sent to the wagon repair depot at Warrington Arpley yard for fitter's attention. The wagon is miscoded as HNNA, but information suggests No. 354947 was in fact a HMA fitted with a canopy and modified braking system.

IWB – 33 80 279 7 702-3 – Peak Forest Up Holding sidings – 23 February 2002
Stabled in the sidings at Peak Forest on a cold winter's Saturday afternoon is this Perrier-branded IWB van. It was originally built in Germany by Linke Hofmann-Busch between 1977 and 1978, one of a batch of thirty-five such vans. The 'Perrier' branding dates from the days when bottled water was imported into the UK via the Channel train-ferry and later via the Channel Tunnel. The van was waiting to return back to Hope works for re-loading.

IWB – 33 80 279 7 683-0 – Peak Forest Up Holding sidings – 23 February 2002
Also at Peak Forest was this weathered IWB bogie van in the yellow, Blue Circle Cement livery with blue lettering and circle logo. Seven vans were repainted for the Moorswater traffic that EWS had won. The Moorswater terminal reused the former English China Clays dries near Liskeard as a distribution terminal from 1999. The last delivery by rail of cement to Moorswater was from Aberthaw (South Wales) in November 2020, when Tarmac closed the terminal.

PCA – BCC 11045 – Peak Forest Up Holding sidings – 20 March 2002
A handful of the 'Metalair' design PCA tanks received the full Blue Circle Cement lettering and logo when they were overhauled at Doncaster for the new Moorswater traffic. This wagon was one of batch built by Powell Duffryn in 1985. Procor also built two batches according to data recorded by the author at Earle's sidings. The wagon builder plates are affixed to the chassis solebar. Used from Hope to various terminals including Dewsbury and Weaste.

TTA – PR 58262 – Peak Forest Up Holding sidings – 20 March 2002
Once loaded tanks had arrived at Peak Forest on the 'Enterprise' working, they were usually parked in the reception siding and when required were moved over to the locomotive fuelling servicing road or the Up Holding sidings. The gas oil was discharged into on-site holding tanks. Empty tankers were shunted back into the sidings and would initially be returned back to Arpley yard. No. PR 58262 was originally built by Norbrit-Pickering in 1967 for lessor BRT.

TUA – PR 70098 – Peak Forest Up Holding sidings – 20 March 2002
Another of the Norbrit-Pickering built TUA tanks, No. PR 70098 was the first in this batch of twenty wagons. Also branded with CAIB lessor stickers. Livery is a faded grey tank barrel with red solebars. Note the yellow lifting lugs projecting out from the solebars. The most important sticker on the barrel is the orange and back HAZCHEM panel – 3Z 1202 which denotes a Class 3 hazard – defined as gas oil or diesel fuel or light heating oil.

ZFV 'Dogfish' – DB993412 – Peak Forest Up Holding sidings – 28 March 1999
This wagon arrived in spring 1999 and is thought to have been deemed to be defective. The wagon was dumped at the end of the Up Holding sidings and remained there until around spring 2014. On 28 March 1999, I observed a Class 37, No. 37013, passing Woodsmoor, near Stockport, hauling a ballast train that included 'Catfish' ZEV and 'Dogfish' ZFV ballast hoppers – maybe this is how the 1957 Metro-Cammell-built 'Dogfish' got to Peak Forest?

PGAs – REDA 14511 and 14510 – Peak Forest Up Holding sidings – 2 June 2002
During 2002, the Redland-owned PGA hopper wagons were used from Dowlow to East Anglia. At weekends the rake was sometimes parked up at Peak Forest. Procor built twenty-three wagons for Tilbury Roadstone in 1980 and used from Merehead quarry in Somerset to Barham in Suffolk. The wagons were later acquired by Redland in 1986 and used with their own PGAs from Mountsorrel quarry. Many of the Lafarge PGA hoppers have now been scrapped.

HMA – 351316 – Peak Forest Up Holding sidings – 2 June 2002
Here we see another example of a HMA coal hopper awaiting the decision to be called to the Warrington Arpley wagon maintenance depot. The original two-axle merry-go-round air-braked coal hopper fleet as constructed amounted to 11,231 wagons built in batches between 1964 and 1981 at three different BR works. HMAs were originally HAAs but now fitted with a modified braking system.

HMA – 355747 – Peak Forest Up Holding sidings – 2 June 2002
With the painted faded data panel obscured by a graffiti tag, the cast wagon plate bolted to the solebar confirms that this is HMA No. 355747. Note the green card that is clipped into the label holder at the left-hand end of the chassis solebar. The green card denotes that the wagon has been inspected at Hope and deemed 'For Repairs'. These labels were issued when wagons required repairs and were safe to travel subject to restrictions.

PCA – PR 10007 – Peak Forest Up Holding sidings – 2 June 2002
This former Procor-owned ex-Cerestar traffic-branded PCA appeared at Peak Forest during summer 2002. I don't know what traffic this wagon was intended for at the time, but powdered lime or cement would seem a logical choice. This wagon had previously been used to trial fly-ash from Longannet coal-fired power station in Scotland to the Blue Circle Cement works at Westbury in June 1997, so perhaps the PCA was on trial from one of the quarries?

TUA – PR 70065 – Peak Forest Up Holding sidings – 2 June 2002
The TUA and TTA gas oil tanks were always interesting to photograph as you never knew what would be parked in the sidings. Here, we see another of the Charles Roberts-built examples, No. PR 70065, originally built in 1973. The TUA class of wagons were a development of the earlier TTA wagons and exploited the 25.5 tonne axle loading limit and longer, stronger chassis and tank barrel designs. Branded 'CARLESS' and with the original <P> Procor logo.

JGA – RMC 17243 – Peak Forest Reception sidings – 21 August 2002
In 1990 a second batch of air-braked bogie hopper wagons for RMC Dove Holes traffic was ordered by RMC, this time from RFS Industries at Doncaster, and twenty-five wagons were built to this 90 t glw slab-sided design. These new wagons joined the original wagons to move stone from Dove Holes to stone terminals such as Salford Hope Street, Ely, Selby, Washwood Heath and Bletchley.

JGA – RMC 13703 – Peak Forest Reception sidings – 21 August 2002
Although RMC had ordered a batch of hopper wagons from Standard Wagon Co., these were not the first to this design. In 1984, Hall Aggregates ordered thirteen 90 t glw bogie hoppers from Standard Wagon Co. Hall Aggregates (then part of RMC Group) moved sea-dredged aggregates from Newhaven to Tolworth and Crawley. In 1996, the wagons were transferred to Dove Holes quarry. The curved ends were added when all thirteen were refurbished.

JGA – RMC 19221 – Peak Forest Reception sidings – 21 August 2002
Further expansion of the Dove Holes based aggregates traffic by RMC saw the need for a
further batch of bogie hopper wagons to join the existing fleet of sixty-two wagons. An order
for twenty-seven new 90 t JGA wagons was placed in 1996 with Tatrastroj Poprad of Slovakia
for delivery in early 1997. The existing RMC-owned JGA hopper fleet was later taken over by
CEMEX of Mexico in 2005.

MEA – 391008 – Peak Forest Reception sidings – 21 August 2002
Here we see one of the original MEA conversions in a much weathered and faded Railfreight
Coal dark grey and yellow livery. The first batch of forty-five wagons using recycled HEA coal
wagon chassis were converted by RFS at Doncaster in 1990 and was followed by a second batch
of thirty-six wagons in 1993, converted by ABB, Crewe works. Note the Barry Galleon wagon
repair depot, Transrail T logo and mixed overhead warning flashes on the bodyside.

MEA – 391126 – Peak Forest Reception sidings – 21 August 2002
The fourth livery on the MEAs was the Mainline Freight blue with yellow top capping livery.
A batch of sixty wagons was converted by RFS Engineering at Doncaster in 1995. These were
initially numbered M391101–391160, but the M prefix as shown here on No. 391126 was later
painted out in EWS ownership. New HSE style overhead flashes have been applied. Note the
small Mainline Freight 'rolling wheels' corporate logo applied to the bottom-right corner.

HAA – 355754 – Peak Forest Up Holding sidings – 19 January 2003
A full load of coal in this HAA wagon suggests there had been a problem with the unloading
mechanism to release the bottom hopper doors. No. 355754 with a freshly painted front-facing
red cradle is seen stabled at Peak Forest. The wagon data panel has recently been repainted and
the 'AYR' lettering denotes that the wagon was maintained by Ayr wagon depot. At this time
coal for Hope came from the New Cumnock opencast site in East Ayrshire.

HMA – 357072 – Peak Forest Up Holding sidings – 19 January 2003
Another defective loaded MGR wagon from Hope seen awaiting transfer to Warrington Arpley is HMA No. 357072, wearing the remnants of the original yellow-framed Railfreight Coal livery with later red patches added. The appearance of the wagon is typical of those in the twilight of its long career. Many of the MGR fleet were either scrapped or converted into MHA spoil wagons, the latter numbering over a thousand wagons.

HDA – 368312 – Peak Forest Up Holding sidings – 19 January 2003
MGR wagons would last in traffic with EWS and its successor DB Schenker until around 2008, when they were withdrawn in favour of the larger capacity HTA 102 t bogie coal hoppers. Coal for Hope Cement works has over the years come from several sites including Scotland, Immingham, and South Wales. At present coal is moved by rail from South Wales by DB Cargo using a rake of eighteen HTA wagons.

CEA – 360726 – Peak Forest Up Holding sidings – 19 January 2003
The CEA covered hopper wagons occasionally turned up at Peak Forest on trials. A batch of forty-four were originally converted from HEA coal hoppers for Loadhaul in 1996 by the addition of sheeted roller covers. They were converted by RFS (Engineering) and in EWS use were used on several flows including roadstone, industrial coal, china clay, calcified seaweed, pelletised rubber fuel, and limestone. This wagon was noted awaiting scrapping at Booth's in 2007.

Peak Forest looking towards Dove Holes quarry – 5 February 2003
An overview of the RMC Dove Holes quarry in February 2003. At the time, this hired Sentinel 0-6-0 diesel-hydraulic shunter was used to marshal and shunt the hopper wagons as required. Different grades of stone are loaded either using a shovel loader from the loading platform on the right or the large over-track hopper loading shed in the background. Nowadays, this is duty done by mainline locomotives hired in by Victa Railfreight.

TTA – PR 57195 – Peak Forest Up Holding sidings – 5 February 2003
This is a former BRT-owned TTA tank. Although the BRT logo has been removed, the wagon is still listed as being in BRT ownership, though in reality lessor CAIB had taken over the BRT fleet. Once part of a batch of wagons built by Pressed Steel Co. in 1966, by 1990 was on hire to Fina and used on diesel fuel flows from Lindsey and Stanlow oil refineries. By the start of 2021, there were only twenty-one TTA petroleum tanks remaining.

TTA – PR 58255 – Peak Forest Up Holding sidings – 5 February 2003
The 46 t TT series of tank wagons were built by several builders during the 1960s with many variations on the original 'monobloc' one-piece design. Wagons have changed owners over the years – many were built for the likes of Shell and British Petroleum and later passed to wagon-leasing companies. Snow-covered No. PR 58255 was built by Powell Duffryn, Cardiff, in 1966 for BRT as No. 57457 but later passed to Procor then CAIB for hire to Total oil traffic.

JHA – NP 19400 – Peak Forest – 5 February 2003
In 1995, National Power decided to invest in their own fleet of new Class 59/2 diesel locomotives and bogie hoppers to serve its coal-fired power stations. A batch of twenty-one limestone hoppers, were built during 1993/4 by Powell Duffryn SA, France. Split into outers (with buffers) and inners (without) these JHAs took limestone from Tunstead to Drax. This is the first numbered wagon No. NP 19400 delivered by the train-ferry in November 1993.

PCA – BCC 10788 – Hope Earle's sidings – 22 March 2003
An increase in cement traffic from Hope in 2003 saw previously stored 'Vee-tanks' reactivated to the operational fleet. A visit to Earle's sidings in March 2003, with permission enabled me to take photographs of the wagons including No. BCC 10788. This was originally built by BREL Ashford works in 1981 and at the time of writing is still listed as being in traffic for Lafarge. Note the triple weld lines running down the tank barrel.

PCA – BCC 10800 – Hope Earle's sidings – 22 March 2003
Also stabled at Earle's sidings on the same date was No. BCC 10800 from the same BREL Ashford-built batch of wagons. Note the differences in number and data panel style compared to No. 10788. Also No. 10800 appears to have originally been fitted with company nameboards judging by the brackets on the side of the tank barrel. The red painted suspension was often applied to the BCC PCA wagons. This wagon is still extant but is stored at present.

PCA – BCC 10873 – Hope Earle's sidings – 22 March 2003
By the late 1980s, APCM/BCC had 780 PCA tanks in operation to three main designs: the 'Vee-tank' version, the twelve French-built CFMF examples and the 'Metalair' straight-barrel tanks. Wagon No. BCC 10873 was originally built by Procor during 1981/2 for cement traffic from Hope, Oxwellmains, Swanscombe or Westbury. Of these works only Hope and Oxwellmains still produce cement. Note the single central weld line on the tank barrel.

MTA – 395237 – Peak Forest – 27 April 2003
As we have already seen with the HEA conversions to MEAs and CEAs, conversion of redundant wagons extended their working life. In this case No. 395237 was formerly a ZRA departmental water tank. However, before becoming ZRA No. DB999106 in 1992, this wagon was a Shell UK-owned TTA No. SUKO 62114 (later 61114) built by Metro-Cammell, Birmingham, in 1965 for bitumen traffic. This infrastructure MTA was still in traffic in early 2021.

MHA – 394549 – Peak Forest – 27 April 2003
To meet the demand for engineering wagons in the late 1990s, a further programme of conversions took place using surplus and condemned MGR coal wagons started by EWS. The conversion entailed the removal of the hopper body and discharge equipment from the chassis. A simple yet robust low-height box body was affixed to the chassis to make the new wagons. 999 wagons were converted initially. This MHA started life as a HAA coal wagon No. 365191.

MFA – 391346 – Peak Forest – 27 April 2003
Having inherited and ordered further MEA wagons, EWS had a fleet of 573 wagons at the end of the century. EWS embarked on a further round of conversions during 2000 to create more ballast/spoil wagons. Donor wagons were MEAs, and work commenced at both Wabtec and Marcroft Engineering. This is a Marcroft conversion, as the excess body height was removed from the bottom of the box body. The original numbers were retained upon conversion.

MFA – 391105 – Peak Forest – 27 April 2003
Donor wagons were drawn from most of the original MEA batches and once the conversion programme was complete, 135 wagons had been reduced in height to 1.13 metres. Initially the MFAs were used in infrastructure traffic in Scotland, but were later mixed with MHA and MTA wagons as required. This faded Mainline Freight blue example has also been converted by Marcroft Engineering. The M prefix before the number has been removed.

ZCA – DC110677 – Peak Forest – 27 April 2003
In British Rail days, revenue earning wagons were often transferred to the Civil Engineers fleet for further use. 800 two-axle OBAs were built by BREL Ashford and Shildon works from 1977 to 1979. From 1982 onwards surplus open wagons including OBAs were transferred to the Civil Engineers fleet and re-coded ZDA 'Bass'. From 1991, OBAs and ZDAs were converted with new steel bodysides and ends to become ZCA 'Sea Urchins' for ballast and spoil traffic.

ZCA – DC460097 – Peak Forest – 27 April 2003
A further scheme started in 1983 to recode SPAs to ZAA 'Pike'. The ZAAs were not modified but many were repainted into Civil Engineers grey and yellow livery. By 1990, damage to the dropside doors when in ballast and spoil traffic was causing problems. Seventy-five ZAAs initially received strengthened sides and the doors welded shut and recoded ZCA 'Seahare'. Some ZCAs were later repainted into Loadhaul livery like No. DC460097, a 'Seahare'.

ZCA – T110256 – Peak Forest – 27 April 2003
Further ZDA wagons were converted into ZCA 'Sea Urchin' wagons during 1995 for Transrail. Twenty wagons were converted by Marcroft Engineering in 1994 and retained their original numbers. However, they received a T prefix replacing the original DC prefix. A further twenty ZCAs followed in 1995, converted by RFS at Doncaster. All these ZCAs were painted into Transrail's plain grey with red top capping and logo. Note the fifteen-leaf spring suspension.

ZCA – M110483 – Peak Forest – 27 April 2003
After the forty wagons had been converted for Transrail, a follow-up batch was ordered by Mainline Freight. Again, OAA and OBA wagons were used as donors and twenty were converted by RFS during 1996 and painted in the blue with yellow capping livery. There were twenty-one different ZCA design codes covering the 786 wagons so converted until the design fell out of favour in larger capacity bogie box wagons and side-tippers from the year 2000 onwards.

HQAs/JJAs – Peak Forest – 27 April 2003
Also, at Peak Forest on the same day as the MFA, MHA, MTA, and ZCAs was this rake of
ten auto-ballaster wagons. The first wagon is one of the newer HQA wagons built new at RFS
Doncaster – No. 380033 – and is marked with the set number 15 too. The next five wagons
are the converted JJAs that were originally KPA 90 t aggregates hoppers; these were Nos GERS
12981, 12964, 12968, 12959 and 12965 – the latter being generator fitted.

JGA – BLI 11704 – Great Rocks Top Yard – 27 April 2003
In 2002, Buxton Lime Industries announced that they were going in invest in a new cement
production facility at Tunstead to replace the existing smaller plant. As part of the investment an
order was placed with Arbel-Fauvet, France to build a fleet of thirty new bogie cement tanks. The
first nine wagons arrived towards the end of April 2003 and No. BLI 11704 is seen parked in the
reception sidings at Great Rocks awaiting acceptance and loaded trials. Taken with permission
of Tarmac Buxton Lime & Cement.

PCA – BCC 10813 – Hope Works branch siding – 14 June 2003
Not all of the Blue Circle 'Vee-tank' fleet of tanks were brought back into service, and some remained in store. For several years five were stored on the works branch between Earle's sidings and the main works. No. BCC 10813 is interesting as it is fitted with a hand-brake lever as opposed to the usual hand wheel. Still thought to be extant and now stored at the back of the cement works. One of a batch of one hundred tanks built by BREL Ashford in 1981.

PCA – BCC 10804 – Hope Works branch siding – 14 June 2003
Another one of the stored wagons on the branch siding was No. BCC 10804 showing signs of long-term storage and peeling paintwork. What looks like a green undercoat can be seen where the grey paint has peeled and flaked away. The shade is reminiscent of the Albright & Wilson livery as applied to long-scrapped older PCAs used in tripolyphosphate chemicals traffic. Also built by BREL Ashford in 1981, original numbers were BCC 10738–10837.

PCA – was BCC 11030 – Hope Works branch siding – 14 June 2003
Now in use as an internal user wagon at Hope Cement works, this chassis was originally part
of a Metalair PCA cement tank No. BCC 11030. At some point, damage has occurred to tank
barrel, and this has led to the wagon being withdrawn and the barrel scrapped. The wooden
planking on the top of the chassis allows equipment or parts to be moved around the works.
Five of the 'Metalair' type PCAs were withdrawn from traffic prior to 2005.

PCA – APCM 10705 – Hope Works branch siding – 14 June 2003
APCM 10705 is the last survivor of a batch of thirty-eight such PCA tanks built by BREL at
Shildon works in 1978/9 only a few years prior to closure in June 1984. After the construction
traffic boom during the 1980s, many of the APCM and BCC wagons were stored, and many
older ones were scrapped and a few stored. The tank is marked 'Water Only' on the white panel
below the black wagon data panel. Suspension unit detail has now faded to pink.

TUA – NACO 74006 – Peak Forest Up Holding sidings – 14 June 2003
This tank wagon is a further example of the 51 t TUA design used to deliver gas oil to Peak Forest. A batch of thirty tanks was built by C.F.P.M, France, during 1980/1 for Carless Solvents Limited traffic. The TUAs later passed into the ownership of wagon lessor NACCO, who continued to operate the tanks in gas oil traffic. The Carless logo has been removed, but the NACCO logo remains. As of 2021, only ten of the wagons remained all in store.

PCA – RC 10033 – Peak Forest Up Holding sidings – 15 July 2003
In 2000, RMC acquired the Rugby Group, which at the time was a leading British cement business. Rugby used the railways to transport its powdered cement products but by the early 1990s this traffic had largely ceased, and the wagons either placed in store or scrapped. A new to rail flow of lime mortar produced at Dove Holes started and was conveyed in fifteen refurbished former Rugby Cement two-axle PCA tank wagons to move the product to Bletchley.

KFA – GMC 92506 – Peak Forest Up Holding sidings – 15 July 2003
This KFA bogie flat wagon loaded with Greater Manchester Waste Authority refuse containers is not a wagon you would expect to see at Peak Forest. At the time, one of the EWS-hauled refuse trains from Northenden was routed via Peak Forest on Saturday afternoons to allow a crew change to take place. This 1981, Remafer, France-built KFA was removed from the train as defective and dumped in the sidings to await repair and onward movement.

JGA – BLI 11716 – Peak Forest – 15 July 2003
The new cement tanks were given the TOPS wagon code JGA, for private owner bogie hopper wagons. Bogie tanks were usually coded JCA or JDA. The wagons were stored in Great Rocks sidings until July. Here we see the return empties from Walsall at Peak Forest heading back to Tunstead. No. BLI 11716 was the only one branded BLI Buxton Cement after a suggestion to BLI just before the Hillhead quarrying exhibition, where the JGA was displayed.

JGAs – Great Rocks Top Yard – 27 September 2003
After the loaded trial to the new Walsall terminal, the Arbel-Fauvet built wagons remained at Great Rocks sidings. By September 2003, all were noted covered with these blue tarpaulin sheets making identification of wagon numbers impossible. The Tunstead cement scheme allowed two more new terminals to be built at Leeds Hunslet and London Willesden too. The overall cost of the scheme was £100 million, of which £11.74 million was from a Freight Facilities Grant.

MJA – 502038 – Hope Earle's sidings – 18 April 2004
Freightliner Heavy Haul introduced a batch of new bogie box wagons in late 2003. Thirty twinsets were built by Greenbrier and numbered Nos 502001–502060. The wagons were joined with a bar coupling with a standard draw hook, screw couplings and buffers on the outer ends. Almost brand-new No. 502038 is seen parked in the Manchester end head shunt at Earle's sidings, paired with No. 502037 out of view. Initially used from Dowlow quarry.

JIA – 33 70 9382 010-4 – Peak Forest Up Holding sidings – 1 May 2004
In 2004 the JIA 'Polybulk' fleet of wagons was owned by wagon lessor VTG and they embarked upon a programme of overhauling their wagons. A new light grey livery replaced the original liveries and smartened the appearance of the wagons up as illustrated. Thirteen wagons were initially overhauled for Potash traffic from Boulby to Middlesborough for VTG. Some of these later ended up in the Dowlow pool of wagons along with four JAA wagons.

PGA – REDA 14796 – Peak Forest Up Holding sidings – 1 October 2004
Left behind in the sidings at Peak Forest is this Lafarge-liveried PGA hopper wagon. Originally built by Standard Wagon Co. in 1985/6, this was one of eleven wagons in this batch. There were three similar batches of wagons built by Standard Wagon between 1978 and 1986 for Redland Aggregates traffics from Mountsorrel. At the time, Freightliner were hiring Lafarge PGAs to convey limestone from Dowlow to various coal-fired power stations.

JHA – ARC 17924 – Peak Forest – 17 March 2005
In addition to the regular aggregates traffic from Dove Holes new short-term flows appeared like this one to Acton in west London. Hanson-owned JHA bogie hopper wagons were used on this flow during 2005. Built by Standard Wagon Co. in 1990 for ARC from Whatley quarry in the Mendips. The JHAs moved limestone aggregates to London and the South-East. This is one the outer wagons built after the prototype Procor-built JHA (JFA) wagons.

JHA – ARC 19822 – Peak Forest – 17 March 2005
The next wagon in the empty train from Acton to Dove Holes was this JHA inner wagon. The Hanson JHAs were marshalled into rakes comprising of an outer buffer fitted wagon, then a series of inner non-buffer fitted wagons and another outer wagons and all coupled together using auto-couplings. ARC 19822 was built by Powell Duffryn-Standard during 1990/1. All of the ex-ARC Hanson wagons were fitted with TF1 low-track force bogies.

HAA – 356809 – Hope Earle's sidings – 30 April 2005
Taken with permission on a wet Saturday in 2005 is this photograph of a HAA coal wagon. At the time, coal was being received at Earle's sidings from New Cumnock opencast site. Located in East Ayrshire on the Glasgow South Western line, this supplied coal to Hope until May 2013 when the opencast site closed. MGR wagons for the flow to Hope were based at Ayr and some received blue painted cradles and the Scottish Saltire, or St Andrew's Cross, too.

HAA – 354425 – Hope Earle's sidings – 30 April 2005
This HAA appears to have a much-faded EWS maroon cradle with a few extra embellishments. Note the black patch with the VIBT (Vehicle Inspection and Brake Test) and PPM (Planned Preventative Maintenance) dates written on. The dates read 29-4-05 and the five-digit code next to the date was for Carlisle area, possibly Kingmoor Yard. VIBT and PPM require visual measurement and inspection to determine the operating condition of wagon.

PCA – BCC 10987 – Hope Earle's sidings – 30 April 2005
On the same wet Saturday, the final Procor-built PCA 'Vee-tank' built in 1982 is parked in the sidings too. Note the large circular weld mark on the domed barrel end. Presumably, this was from a repair that was needed to keep the wagon in traffic. The tank beyond has a similar but smaller weld repair too. Note the Wabtec Rail white sticker below the data panel. This wagon is one of 236 PCAs recorded as active at the start of 2021, with a further twenty stored.

MCA – 500233 – Peak Forest Up Holding sidings – 18 June 2005
After delivery of the 300 Thrall Europa-built MBA 'Monster Box' wagons, a decision was made to reduce the height on the last 100 wagons. Difficulties were encountered at certain locations when trying to load or unload the wagons. The final 100 numbered wagons, Nos 500201 to 300, were split into two types; the first forty becoming MCAs with drawgear and buffers fitted at both ends. Here is No. 500232 loaded with fresh ballast.

MDA – 500275 – Peak Forest Up Holding sidings – 18 June 2005
The remainder of the 100 ex-MBA wagons were converted in the same manner at the Thrall Europa works to become sixty MDA inner wagons that only had auto-couplers fitted. They were numbered 500241 to 500300. The MCA and MDAs were initially used for infrastructure work in semi-fixed rakes in connection with the West Coast Main Line upgrade work. A batch of fifty similar new wagons coded MOA were also built in 2003 in the Czech Republic.

PGAs – Hope Earle's sidings – 2 July 2005
After the hiring in Lafarge wagons for the Dowlow to power stations limestone traffic, Freightliner turned to VTG for further PGAs. Here we see three of the former CAIB-owned PGAs left to right, Nos VTG 14456, 14434 and 14288. These were in a rake of thirty-three PGAs stabled at Earle's sidings along with three more PGAs stopped for repairs. Some of these PGAs were previously used on the Tunstead to Northwich limestone traffic between 1998 and 2001.

PGA – VTG 14722 – Hope Earle's sidings – 2 July 2005
The rake has been loaded up at Dowlow and is stabled in the sidings at Hope for the weekend. This wagon was one of a batch of twenty-nine built by Procor, Wakefield in 1978/9 for ARC aggregates traffic from Whatley and Tytherington quarries. These wagons would last several more years in traffic before being stored pending scrapping. Note the freshly applied notices on black backgrounds, the Procor logo, and the original Procor P plate on the solebar.

PGA – VTG 14714 – Hope Earle's sidings – 2 July 2005
Another PGA wagon from the same builder also originally built for ARC aggregates traffic. Livery is probably best described as rusty ARC mustard brown. Note the different style of top lip compared to No. VTG 14722. The differences are reflected in the original TOPS design codes; PG 013A for 14714 (fifteen wagons Nos 14706–720) and PG 013B for 14722 (twenty-nine wagons Nos 14721–749). The hired PGAs were later replaced by new bogie hoppers.

Hope Cement works sidings – 2 July 2005
This 2005 view of the main sidings at Hope shows the main three wagon types that were in use at the time; the EWS-owned MGR coal wagons to the left and middle, followed by two rakes of mostly PCA 'Vee-tanks' and then two rakes of the IWB Cargowaggon bogie vans outside the bagged products loading warehouse. The original works layout beyond was rather cramped and some years later was redesigned, and new sidings laid for increased traffic output.

JMA – NP 19681 – Peak Forest – 5 August 2005
After EWS took over the National Power fleet in 1998, the JMA coal hoppers were tried in traffic originating from Liverpool Bulk Terminal taking coal to the Fiddler's Ferry power station. A pool of twenty-five wagons (six JHAs and nineteen JMAs) worked from Tunstead in aggregates and limestone traffic alongside the JHA hoppers. The JMAs were built at National Power's depot in Ferrybridge from a kit of parts supplied by OY Transtech of Finland.

BRA – 964002 – Peak Forest Up Holding sidings – 13 November 2005
This BRA covered steel slab wagon has been sent to Peak Forest for use as a coupling adaptor with the JHA and JMA hoppers. The EWS Class 66 locomotives are fitted with American AAR auto-couplers, draw-hooks, and buffers from new. Older classes like 56s, 58s and 60s only had draw-hook couplings and buffers fitted. The BRAs had both types of couplings fitted along with buffers. Fifty BRA wagons were built in 1998 at the Thrall Europa works in York.

TTA – BRT 57210 – Peak Forest Up Holding sidings – 13 November 2005
This TTA was also built by Pressed Steel Co. in 1966 for British Rail Traffic & Electric Company (BRT), who were a leading British wagon lessor from the 1950s to late 1980s. The assets of BRT became part of the Belgian-owned CAIB leasing company. A look at the published data for the TT design of 46 t tanks shows that ten different wagon builders were producing the wagons from the 1960s onwards into the 1970s, when the larger TUAs were introduced.

HIA – 369003 – Buxton Up Reception sidings – 11 February 2006
The privatised freight companies like EWS and Freightliner invested heavily in new freight wagons to meet demand and in some cases new-to-rail flows. A £4 million investment by Freightliner in 2005 saw twenty-three surplus RH Roadstone JGA bogie hoppers acquired and refurbished, plus forty-eight brand-new HIA bogie-hopper wagons built by Greenbrier's Polish Wagon Swidnica works. This rake of wagons were returning to Dowlow quarry for reloading.

HIA – 369035 – Peak Forest – 5 April 2006
The forty-eight new HIA 90 t wagons were delivered by early 2006 and was split into two liveries; twenty-one in Freightliner green intended for spot hire flows and twenty-seven in white, Nos 369022–48. The white livery denoted they were for traffic originating from Tarmac's Tunstead quarry. The first twenty-one wagons, Nos 369001–21, were used from Dowlow – though in operation the two liveries soon started to be mixed together.

FAA – 609071 – Peak Forest Up Holding sidings – 4 June 2006
Another unusual wagon that turned up at Peak Forest in 2006 was this EWS FAA bogie well container wagon. A batch of 100 were built by Thrall Europa during 1999. FAAs were designed to take either two 20-foot or one 40-foot shipping containers in 8-foot 6-inch-high and the slightly larger 9-foot 9-inch-high variants. Why this wagon was at Peak Forest is not known but it is possible it was used as a translator wagon, as the BRA/BYA wagons were.

JHA – NP 19405 – Peak Forest Up Holding sidings – 26 July 2006
In 1995, National Power decided to invest in their own fleet of new Class 59/2 diesel-electric locomotives and bogie limestone and coal hoppers to serve its coal-fired power stations. A batch of twenty-one bogie limestone hoppers were built during 1993/4 by Powell Duffryn SA, France. Split into outers (with buffers) and inners (without) these JHAs took limestone from Tunstead to Drax. Here, inner wagon No. NP 19405 is parked in the sidings on its own.

PAA – WBB 30043 – Peak Forest Up Holding sidings – 27 July 2006
Sand wagons were another unusual visitors to the Peak District. This WBB Minerals-liveried PAA covered sand hopper is seen tagged on rear of a loaded train of MBA boxes bound for Peterborough. The wagon might have been returning from repair at Marcroft Engineering at Stoke-on-Trent and it was just easiest to send via Warrington Arpley and Peak Forest. This was the only occasion I saw a PAA wagon, and all these type wagons have now been scrapped.

TTA – PR 58256 – Peak Forest Reception sidings – 27 July 2006
This TTA tank wagon was originally built by Norbrit-Pickering, Wishaw, 1967 was initially numbered, BRT 57511 on TOPS in the 1970s. It was originally allocated to Total traffic from Lindsey Oil Refinery, which is located in north Lincolnshire not far from Grimsby. Lindsey is now operated by the Prax Group, a British multinational independent oil refining company. Note the Railfreight Petroleum logo sticker applied to the tank barrel on the right-hand side.

HOAs and JGAs – Great Rocks Top Yard – 8 April 2007
In 2007 EWS Construction introduced a new fleet of sixty-eight 90 t HOA aggregates wagons. These were built by Trinity Rail (later IRS), at the Astra Vagoane works, Romania in 2006. The HOAs were used from Stud Farm and East Usk quarries (aggregates) and Marks Tey and Middleton Towers (sand). By March 2007, six new HOA wagons were being trialled out of Tunstead including Nos 320000, 01, 04, 06 and 15. A rake of BLI JGA tanks is parked in front.

HOA – 320038 – Peak Forest Reception sidings – 7 May 2007
Once the new fleet of sixty-eight HOA 90 t aggregates wagons had been delivered, they soon arrived in the Peak District, initially on trial from Tunstead as we have seen. Initially, they were used on the Tunstead to Bredbury/Pendleton aggregates traffic but soon after were sent to work from Dove Holes quarry. The HOAs and the next batch of new wagons, the IIAs displaced the former RMC JGA fleet, were by then owned by EWS Construction.

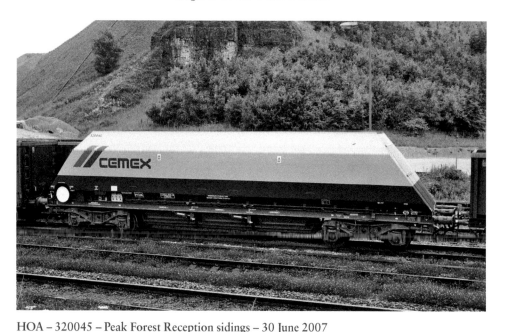

HOA – 320045 – Peak Forest Reception sidings – 30 June 2007
EWS Construction quickly moved to repaint forty-eight of their new HOA hoppers into a
CEMEX-branded livery in connection with a new six-year railfreight deal. Wagons were
repainted at the Marcroft wagon works at Stoke-on-Trent for traffic out of Dove Holes. Here
newly painted, No. 320045 is marshalled between EWS MBA and MEA wagons having arrived
from Stoke via the 'Enterprise' wagonload service from Warrington Arpley yard.

JPA – VTG 12401 – Hope Earle's sidings – 23 July 2007
Some 'gen' from a fellow wagon enthusiast, led to me visiting Earles sidings early one morning in
July 2007 to capture this photograph of brand-new JPA bogie cement tank No. VTG 12401. The
wagon had been delivered a few days earlier and this was the first test-run to Hull and Derby
and back. This was the first of forty-eight wagons built for Lafarge, who then owned Hope
Cement works. The wagons were built in Germany by Feldbinder to a new design.

PCA – BCC 10787 – Hope Cement works wagon repair shops – 26 January 2008
By 2008, Freightliner Heavy Haul had taken over the maintenance of the PCA wagon fleet from Lafarge. Most wagons had a small Freightliner Heavy Haul white sticker applied below the wagon data panel. Hope Cement works has a modern wagon repair workshop that enables repairs, parts, and exams to be carried out on the wagon fleet when they are due, usually every six months. Note the green card in the clip holder denoting this wagon needs attention.

JHA – NP 19408 – Peak Forest Up Holding sidings – 10 February 2008
This is a former National Power JHA limestone hopper, now in EWS ownership. After only four years, National Power sold its fleet of Class 59/2 locomotives, and the twenty-one JHAs along with the eighty-five larger JMA bogie coal hoppers. The wagons soon moved onto other duties including from Tunstead quarry to Bredbury and Pendleton stone terminals. At least seven of the JHAs received this partial repaint into EWS maroon on the flat bodyside panel as seen here.

HIA – 369028 – Tunstead Bottom sidings – 21 April 2008
I was fortunate to be granted an official visit to Tunstead quarry in connection with some research I was doing at the time. Our guide showed around the works and included the main sidings too. Here we see one of the white-liveried Freightliner Heavy Haul HIA hoppers bringing up the rear of a loaded rake. This wagon, No. 369028, was one of twenty-four that would eventually depart Tunstead bound for Ratcliffe Power Station. Taken with permission of Tarmac Buxton Lime & Cement.

HIA – 369006 – Tunstead Bottom sidings – 21 April 2008
Also, in the rake of HIAs loaded with fine limestone for Ratcliffe Power Station was this green-liveried HIA No. 396006. Approximately 340,000 tonnes/annum of crushed limestone is used at Ratcliffe to de-sulphurise the flue gas emissions. The Tunstead limestone is used to make a slurry, which helps capture the unwanted sulphur dioxide and converts to calcium sulphite and carbon dioxide and eventually calcium sulphate – commonly known as gypsum. Taken with permission of Tarmac Buxton Lime & Cement.

JEA – BM 19704 – Tunstead Bottom sidings – 21 April 2008
Just over seven years after the JEA hoppers had been introduced, the crimson Brunner Mond crescent logo had all but faded on the wagons. In 2006, the Indian global company Tata bought Brunner Mond and later rebranded as Tata Chemicals Europe. No new livery was applied and the fleet was later acquired by DB Schenker during 2015. The wagons remain in the same condition today, used solely on the Northwich limestone traffic. Taken with permission of Tarmac Buxton Lime & Cement.

JGA – BLI 11729 – Tunstead works wagon repair shops – 21 April 2008
At the time of this visit in 2008, Tarmac Buxton Lime & Cement operated a wagon maintenance shed on site, allowing repairs and inspections of their wagons to take place. Here, a pair of the JGA cement tanks including No. BLI 11729 have been stopped for examination. The white numbers and markings applied to the JGAs were soon obscured when in traffic and covered with cement dust. Note the two-digit 29 repeater number on the barrel end dome. Taken with permission of Tarmac Buxton Lime & Cement.

JGA – RMC 17234 – Peak Forest Long sidings – 3 July 2008
The former RMC JGA fleet continued to work out of Dove Holes quarry for a while until the HOA and IIA fleets had been introduced. The JGAs were then used in traffic from the Midlands and Mendips quarries. Many of the JGAs had the RMC diamond logos and the roadstone branding painted out – some wagons retained their logos intact. Note the EWS maroon painted axle-box covers. Many of the former RMC JGA wagons have since been scrapped.

JPA – VTG 12410 – Hope Cement works sidings – 6 September 2008
After a year or so in traffic, the JPA bogie tankers still looked remarkably clean considering the dusty nature of the cement powder loads. Taken from a passing shuttle train at the 2008 works open day, this is No. VTG 12410. A further fifteen JPA tanks were built as a follow-on order and went new to Castle Cement for Anglo-Scottish traffic. Further batches of JPA Uacns cement tank wagons were built for Hope Construction Materials, Colas/Tarmac, VTG/Hanson and VTG/Tarmac.

JNA – VTG 3473 – Peak Forest Up Holding sidings – 27 September 2008
Following on from the MEA and MJAs box wagons, the CAIB-owned fleet of JNA boxes were also used on aggregates traffic from Dowlow and Dove Holes. A fleet of 120 wagons were built by Marcroft Engineering in 1998 using second-hand bogies. Initially the fleet was used on Railtrack 'virtual quarry' rail ballast traffic around the country. After this traffic ended the wagons returned to lessor CAIB, who decided to refurbish their JNA fleet for further use.

Various wagons – Dove Holes CEMEX quarry sidings – 28 September 2008
Looking over the fence and into Dove Holes quarry sidings, we see most of the wagon types pictured so far. In the foreground is a CEMEX-branded rake of the nearly new IIA 90 t hopper wagons. In the background a rake of seven PCA tanks are parked outside the wagon repair shed along with a trio of 1997-built JGAs. A mixed rake of JGAs and HOAs completes the line-up.

IIA – 33 70 6955 098-2 – Dove Holes CEMEX quarry sidings – 28 September 2008
The IIA bogie hopper wagons were built by Greenbrier Europe at the Wagony Swidnica works in Poland during 2008 for EWS Construction. These IIA wagons were delivered new in the grey and blue CEMEX-branded livery. The thirty-four wagons are numbered in the RIV number series 33 70 6955 068–101 (thus continuing on from HOA 320067) range as wagon designation Fabfnoos. The new fleet now totalled 102 HOA and IIA wagons.

JRA – 33 70 6790 013-0 – Peak Forest – 17 January 2009
Most rail traffic from Dove Holes uses bogie hopper wagons, but some flows used two-axle and bogie open box wagons. In 1988, wagon lessor Tiphook Rail introduced a new design of bogie open box wagons coded JRA, built by French builder Arbel Fauvet. On this occasion, JRA wagons were being used to take raw crushed limestone from Dove Holes to West Burton power station, the train seen departing Peak Forest just after 1 p.m. in the afternoon.

HOA – 320014 – Peak Forest – 15 March 2009
By early 2009, many of the HOA and IIA CEMEX-branded wagons had the CEMEX logo crudely painted out as shown. The effects of stone spillage, traffic dust and dirt has taken its toll on the paintwork as is common with most wagons after year or so in service. The HOAs and IIAs were used on the same duties from Dove Holes. As traffic and demand changed the wagons eventually moved away onto other aggregate flows from the Midlands and Mendips.

IIA – 33 70 6955 070-1 – Peak Forest – 15 March 2009
The IIA wagons were also de-branded in the same manner as the HOAs. The solebar on the IIA wagons is adorned with various dimensions, notices and lettering that reads 'Provided by EWS Construction'. The HOA and IIA wagons are fitted with the same design of TF25 low track-force bogies too. Similar IIA wagons were built for Mendip Rail/NACCO (forty wagons) and then Mendip Rail/VTG (twenty). Like the HOAs, still in traffic from Dove Holes.

JGA – RMC 19222 – Peak Forest Reception sidings – 28 June 2009
Another example of the de-branded former RMC JGA wagons is seen parked in the Reception
Siding. No. 19222 has had the RMC diamond logo and the 'roadstone' lettering neatly painted
out black. Although the JGAs were now owned by EWS, the owners code RMC was never
changed. Seven wagons from this batch Nos 19220–19225, plus 19239, are known to have the
'roadstone' lettering from new. A pool of JGAs were retained for Dove Holes traffic.

MEAs – Peak Forest – 5 July 2009
Occasionally, it is necessary to clean out railway wagons, especially the open box types. Cleaning
out of unwanted stone, dust and general debris may be required if the wagons are to be used
on a new flow. It is important there is no cross-contamination that may for example affect a
chemical process used by the customer. Definitely a job for a quiet Sunday sees a rake of MEAs
being cleaned out assisted by Volvo Excavator and operator.

JRA – 33 70 6790 048-6 – Peak Forest Reception sidings – 30 April 2010
After many years of intensive use around the UK on aggregates and later scrap traffic, the former Tiphook Rail JRA box wagons were looking somewhat tatty. Only one wagon was painted into the revised Tiphook Rail blue livery. Over time, the numbers, data, warning, and instructions all become faded and obscured. This wagon has received new freshly painted black patches and RIV markings plus yellow ferry lashing rings and used from Dove Holes quarry.

JNA – VTG 3511 – Hindlow Brigg's sidings – 12 June 2010
The Railtrack/CAIB JNA wagons reused bogies and brake fittings obtained from scrapped petroleum and powder tank wagons. ESC bogies with clasp shoe brakes and several types of Gloucester bogies with clasp shoe and disc brakes were reused. Here is No. VTG 3511 fitted with Gloucester bogies and disc brakes. It is seen passing Brigg's sidings heading to Dowlow Lafarge where the JNAs will be reloaded with aggregates for Ashburys near Manchester.

JNA – VTG 3464 – Hindlow Brigg's sidings – 12 June 2010
After being replaced by newer Network Rail high-capacity bogie box wagons, CAIB, who owned the JNA wagons, overhauled and modified the fleet for non-ballast traffic. Modifications included a revised top capping, corners, and access hatches in the sides to allow stone, debris to be swept out. Seen passing Hindlow Brigg's sidings ground frame from Peak Forest, where the empty rake of JNAs had been stabled overnight having returned back from Ashburys.

JGA – VTG 19210 – Great Rocks – 21 August 2010
By 2010, the Buxton Lime Industries wagon fleet had been acquired by wagon lessor, VTG, a deal, which saw them take over the operation and maintenance of the wagons at Tunstead. All twenty limestone hoppers were repainted into a plain white livery, with a dark blue VTG logo positioned at the left-hand end. Two wagons (Nos 19203 and 207) had the logo at the right-hand end. This is No. VTG 19210 waiting to depart Great Rocks with a load for Hindlow.

JRA – 33 70 6790 041-1 – Peak Forest – 9 June 2011
The JRAs were built to RIV standards built by French wagon builder, Arbel-Fauvet between 1988 and 1990. JRA wagons were used on aggregates flows from Dove Holes and Dowlow and occasionally limestone from Tunstead. Aggregates produced by the quarries in the Peak District can be split into several main types all suitable for roadstone and construction projects and all can be transported by rail in hopper or open box wagons.

TTAs – Peak Forest Reception sidings - 9 June 2011
By 2011, the supply of gas oil to Peak Forest for the locomotive fuelling and servicing point had switched to Esso and so the CAIB-owned TTA and TUA tanks were no longer used. Here, a pair of TTAs, Nos ESSO 56109 and 56121, have been dropped off by the Warrington Arpley to Dowlow trip working. The ESSO-owned TTA tankers were kept a lot cleaner than the CAIB wagons barring the usual fuel spillage down the barrel sides.

JGA – RMC 19232 – Great Rocks – 9 June 2011
To bolster the VTG fleet of limestone hoppers used on the traffic from Tunstead to Hindlow,
Bredbury and Pendleton, EWS-allocated eleven JGA wagons to a spot hire pool to help out.
This wagon and another ex-RMC JGA, No. RMC 17221, were given a plain grey coat of paint,
possibly to cover up offensive graffiti. This is No. RMC 19232 in the middle of a rake of empty
hoppers from Hindlow parked in Down and Up Through Goods loop.

PBA (JAA) – VTG 13521 – Peak Forest Reception sidings – 7 April 2012
The 1983 Cadoux-built PBA bogie covered hoppers had been used on the flow of powdered
lime from Dowlow to Mossend since the early 1980s. Originally, twenty-five wagons were built
for Tiger Rail and used on a variety of flows. Some wagons later had the top cover removed and
became PHA hoppers. Only five PBA wagons survived the collapse of Tiger Rail in 1992. Four
were retained for the Dowlow to Mossend traffic and all were later scrapped.

TTA – ESSO 56194 – Peak Forest Up Holding sidings – 7 April 2012
An ex-works ESSO TTA is waiting to depart Peak Forest having discharged the payload of gas oil into the EWS storage tanks. Livery is plain grey with no owner markings and a red solebar and axle-box covers. A batch of 200 tanks were built in 1965 by Norbrit-Pickering for traffic from ESSO's Fawley refinery. Nowadays, gas oil is delivered by road tanker to Peak Forest and similar smaller depots, only the larger ones still receiving bulk deliveries by rail.

JGA – RMC 17207 – Peak Forest – 18 March 2013
Although the former RMC JGA wagons had been transferred away from Dove Holes, they did occasionally reappear at Peak Forest. Still wearing the RMC owner prefix, No. 17207 is mixed in with former EWS HOA and IIA hoppers in this rake of empties arriving back at Peak Forest from the Hope Street terminal in Salford. Some of the RMC 192xx numbered JGAs saw further use working out of Tunstead along with the similar BLI later VTG JGA hoppers.

OAA – 100076 – Peak Forest Reception sidings – 25 June 2013
For a short time, concrete blocks were conveyed by rail from Dove Holes quarry. EWS supplied mesh-sided OAA and OBA wagons for this traffic as required. Here we see one of the OAA wagons dumped at the end of the siding on the buffer stop. Originally fitted with wooden planked drop-side doors, EWS converted many of these to a much lighter and stronger metal mesh-side as shown, retaining the original ends. Note the skeletal chassis framework.

JGA – ERG 17324 – Peak Forest – 25 June 2013
GBRf started taking stone from the Peak District during 2013. A loaded Tunstead to Brentford train passes Peak Forest behind a First GB Railfreight Class 66. A batch of twenty-seven PHAs were built by W.H. Davis in 1987 for R.H. Roadstone Limited. Now coded JGA, Freightliner acquired the remaining twenty-three wagons and overhauled them. Lessor ERG took over and de-branded/repainted the JGAs for use by GBRf, but all have now been scrapped.

PCA – BCC 10842 – Hope Cement works sidings – 6 September 2008
A small batch of twelve PCA tanks were built by French builder C.F.M.F. in 1980. These tanks tended to work from the Dunbar (Oxwellmains) works but have occasionally worked from Hope too. No. 10842 was spotted in the sidings from the passing open day shuttle train. Two similar batches to this tank design were built for lessor STS, the first by C.F.M.F. in 1982 (fifty-two wagons) followed by another smaller batch in 1985 built by Fauvet Girel, France (fifteen wagons).

HOA – 320013 – Peak Forest Reception sidings – 25 March 2015
By 2015, the HOA wagons had been in service nearly eight years and EWS Construction had become DB Schenker in January 2009. This HOA No. 320013 had recently been overhauled at the Axiom wagon repair and maintenance facility at Stoke-on-Trent. The bogies appear to have been cleaned and painted grey, but the buffers are DB red. HOA No. 320054 was the first to be repainted by Axiom Rail at Stoke at the end of 2014.

MBA – 500129 – Peak Forest Up Holding sidings – 25 March 2015
This inner MBA wagon fitted only with auto-coupler drawgear and no buffers is parked in the sidings looking rather weather beaten after sixteen years in traffic. Note the 'Wrekin' logo sticker under the EWS lettering. Wrekin Construction used fly-ash from Drax power station and railed to Northwich. Fly-ash was mixed with cement making a slurry and pumped into old underground salt caverns. The 'Startrak' self-weighing control panel is mounted underneath.

MJAs – 502054 – Peak Forest – 27 March 2015
Another flow that GBRf started was from Tunstead to Wellingborough. This initially used a rake of hired CAIB JNA green-liveried box wagons. By 2015, this flow was using a rake of ex-Freightliner MJA twin-box wagons. All sixty wagons used as thirty twin-box sets were now owned by the wagon lessor and de-branded. Here a rake of MJAs passes Peak Forest South signal box climbing up to the line summit en route to Wellingborough.

JXA – VTG 3121 – Stockport – 31 March 2015

Wagon lessor VTG of Germany acquired the wagon fleets of other lessors and private companies from 2002 onwards and gradually built up a large fleet of UK-based wagons as VTG Rail UK. This included several designs of bogie box wagons originally built for Sheerness Steel scrap traffic in the 1980s. Here, one of the refurbished JXAs, No. VTG 3121, is seen passing through Stockport station one morning returning empty from Ashburys to Dowlow.

JXA – VTG 3151 – Stockport – 31 March 2015

Also, in the same Ashburys to Dowlow empty rake was another VTG-owned JXA wagon. This wagon was one of a batch of ten such wagons built by Procor for Sheerness Steel traffic in 1986 at the works in Wakefield. As is often the case if a wagon can be repurposed then a use will be found for it. The JXAs, JRAs and JNAs worked these services until the DB Cargo owned MMA boxes came into traffic in late 2016.

JGA – VTG 11713 – Hazel Grove – 26 April 2015
Following the VTG takeover, the JGA cement tanks were gradually overhauled and repainted into a new livery. Now branded Tarmac Buxton Lime and Cement in plain grey with green and yellow stripes at one end only. No. VTG 11713 is seen passing Hazel Grove after leaving Tunstead one Sunday afternoon near the start of the long journey to the Westbury distribution terminal.

HTA – 310406 – Peak Forest Long sidings – 10 May 2015
In October 2001, the UK government implemented the European Union Large Combustion Plant Directive (LCPD) policy. The aim of the LCPD was to reduce carbon emissions throughout Europe. The effect on the UK coal-fired power stations was immense. DB Schenker quickly found itself with a large fleet of bogie ex-EWS HTA coal hoppers with little or no work to do. Sets of HTA wagons were trialled in aggregates traffic out of Dove Holes from early 2015.

HTA – 310775 – Peak Forest Long sidings – 10 May 2015
Also, in the same rake of HTA wagons this day was this de-branded HTA, where the large EWS gold lettering has been painted out. Not all of the HTAs were de-branded, and many were wearing their full EWS maroon and gold livery right to the end. The large flat sides did prove to be targets for the attention of the graffiti community over time. By 2021, many redundant HTAs were stored, and many have now been sent for scrap by DB Cargo.

HTA – 310374 – Hope Earle's sidings – 23 June 2015
By August 2010, Hope was the last works to receive coal in MGR wagons. This changed to using sets of HTA wagons instead. However, due to the steeply graded works branch and cramped unloading facilities, rakes are formed as three sets of six wagons. The outer wagons of each set are buffer fitted to allow the works' Class 20 to couple up. At present coal comes from Cwmbargoed opencast colliery in South Wales twice a week hauled by DB Cargo.

JPA – VTG 12400 – Hope Earle's sidings – 23 June 2015
Nearly eight years after delivery, the first of the forty-eight JPA tanks delivered for Lafarge traffic is seen at Earles sidings heading back to the works for reloading. Twenty-three of this batch transferred to Lafarge later Tarmac traffic out of nearby Tunstead works, while the remaining twenty-five stayed working from Hope. When Lafarge Tarmac split in 2012, Hope Cement works passed to a management buy-out named Hope Construction Materials.

MUA – 900241 – Peak Forest Long sidings – 24 June 2015
In 2015, three surplus bogie steel wagons, a BAA, BLA and BDA were stripped down and fitted with a new low-sided box body suitable for loading with stone, railway ballast and other bulk materials. This MUA is seen on the rear of a loaded Dove Holes to Attercliffe, Sheffield service. Only one BAA steel carrier was converted to a MUA. The BAA was built by BREL at Ashford works in 1975 and converted by W.H. Davis in 2015.

MVA – 910164 – Dove Holes quarry sidings – 24 June 2015
The second conversion that W.H. Davis completed for DB Schenker was to make a BLA 74 t bogie coil carrier into a MVA with a similar but longer body than the previous MUA conversion. Seen here in the quarry sidings at Dove Holes in a rake destined for Attercliffe stone terminal just east of Sheffield. The third conversion using the BDA 58 t steel carriers were more successful. Over 200 BDAs were converted to MXAs by Axiom Rail at Stoke.

PCA – RC 10038 – Peak Forest Up Holding sidings – 24 June 2015
After several years in traffic conveying lime mortar from Dove Holes to Bletchley, the fleet of fifteen orange tanks gradually dropped out of traffic once EWS Construction then DB took control of the former RMC wagon fleet. Fourteen tanks were stored in the Up Holding sidings from June 2015 onwards. By April 2019 just two tanks remained, and they were taken away by road for scrap soon after.

MEA – 391668 – Peak Forest Up Holding sidings – 24 June 2015
By 1998, EWS had 573 MEAs in traffic. Conversions of MEAs to MFAs started in 2001 and 135 MFAs were converted by cutting the body height down by around two-thirds. In early 2004, EWS authorised the conversion of a new batch of 100 surplus HEAs into MEAs by Wabtec of Doncaster. However, only the first sixty-eight wagons were actually converted. The paintwork on this batch did not last as well as the previous MEAs.

HTAs – Peak Forest Reception sidings – 26 October 2015
Given that limestone is denser than coal, the HTA wagons were never filled to the top. As you can see the looking inside the wagons, they were usually loaded to between just over half and two-thirds full. This depended on how the wagon was loaded, either by shovel or under the loading bunker. Both methods are used to load hopper and box wagons, and this will involve several shunting moves to fully load a train, which makes for interesting viewing at Peak Forest.

JPAs – Peak Forest – 26 October 2015
After the demerger of the short-lived Lafarge Tarmac company in 2012, twenty-three of the forty-eight JPA tanks transferred to Tarmac traffic from Tunstead works. The JPAs worked alongside the existing JGA cement tanks but to my knowledge the two designs were not mixed together. Here a rake of twenty-two JPA is seen passing Peak Forest shortly after departure from Tunstead forming a loaded service to the then new West Thurrock terminal.

JXA – VTG 3125 – Peak Forest Up Holding sidings – 7 February 2016
VTG JXA box wagons were used from Dove Holes and Dowlow until the end of 2016, when the new DB MMA boxes started to arrive from Romania. There were several similar batches of JXA bogie box wagons built by Procor, Wakefield between 1982 and 1987. Wagon No. VTG 3125 was one of forty built as two versions – thirty (Nos 3100–3129) built with short boxes with angled end spill plates and the final ten (3130–3139) with full-length box bodies.

JNA – GERS 4403 – Peak Forest – 13 March 2016

Box wagons were the favourite option for railfreight operators especially for short-term contract flows. Two designs of high-capacity box wagons were brought in to work from Dove Holes and Dowlow. GERS shortly after became part of Touax Global Rail Services. The twenty-six wagons, Nos GERS 4400–25, were built new by W.H. Davis in 2002 reusing parts from former bogie petroleum tankers.

JNA – TIPH 9830 – Peak Forest – 13 March 2016

The other design of bogie open box wagons used were these ex-Tiphook-owned JNAs. Thirty-six wagons, Nos TIPH 9800–35, were built by Marcroft Engineering during 1997 for Allied Steel & Wire scrap traffic. These reused the underframes from redundant Railease/Clyde Cement PBA bogie powdered cement tankers. These TIPH wagons also passed into Touax ownership as well when in use from Dove Holes CEMEX and Dowlow Lafarge.

HRA – 41 70 6723 001-7 – Peak Forest Reception sidings – 14 July 2017
The Thrall Europa-built HTA hopper wagons were used for the CEMEX traffic from Dove Holes quarry for just over three years. To try and overcome the issue of wagon capacity, DB authorised the conversion of HTA No. 310711 by shortening the wagon by one discharge bay to create the HRA wagon. Here the prototype HRA is coupled to a rake of HTAs when it was on trial out of Dove Holes. The wagon was converted by Axiom Rail in summer 2017.

BYA – 966254 – Peak Forest Reception sidings – 14 July 2017
We have already seen one of the BRA ex-EWS sliding hood bogie steel carriers at Peak Forest in 2005. Now that the redundant HTA coal hoppers were being used on aggregates traffic, there was a need for a convertor wagon again. This was to allow the non-auto coupler fitted Class 60s to haul the HTA and HRA hopper wagons. The 260 BYA covered coil carrier wagons were built by Thrall Europa at York in 1999.

HTA and HRA – Peak Forest Reception sidings – 14 July 2017
A total of 1,144 HTA coal hoppers were originally built for EWS and eventually 110 were converted and shortened by 20 per cent by the removal of one hopper bay to become HRA wagons. A rake of twenty-seven HRAs allows an increase of 447 tonnes payload for the same length when compared to standard rake of twenty-two HTAs that were being used. HTA 310504 and HRA 41 70 6723 001-7 illustrate the changes to the wagons before and after.

JGA – RMC 17245 – Peak Forest Up Holding sidings – 30 October 2017
Only four of the original eighty-nine orange and white former RMC JGAs received a repaint into the DB Schenker red livery as worn by No. 17245. Seen parked in the Up Holding sidings while awaiting repairs. The other three known wagons are Nos 13704, 17231 and 19232. The first few months of 2021 saw twenty-three of the now surplus JGAs sent for scrap. The British operations of DB Schenker were rebranded as DB Cargo UK in March 2016.

MMA – 81 70 5500 392-2 – Peak Forest Reception sidings – 30 October 2017
Towards the end of 2016, DB Cargo authorised the construction of a new generation of bogie box wagons intended to replace the MEA two-axle box wagons and the larger MBA 102 t box wagons. The move away from the traditional two-axle wagons was well underway by the mid-2010s. Two batches totalling 166 wagons were built by Astra Rail of Romania between 2016 and 2017 for DB Cargo. Used on flows from Dowlow and Dove Holes quarries.

HTA – 310001 – Peak Forest Reception sidings – 7 June 2018
The first of the former EWS HTA coal hopper fleet is seen some seventeen years after it was first built, not quite as shiny new when it emerged from Thrall Europa's York works in 2001. When GB Railfreight won the contract for hopper traffic from CEMEX Dove Holes in 2018, rakes of the HTAs were initially used. Some wagons were already de-branded, others had the EWS lettering painted out. Note the deeper gold band around the hopper top.

HHA – 370368 – Peak Forest – 7 June 2018
Until early 2018, traffic from Dove Holes quarry was hauled by EWS and its DB successors. Freightliner won a short-term contract to move aggregates too. In a similar move to DB, Freightliner chose to reuse its former HHA bogie coal hoppers for this traffic. This rake of HHAs is just arriving empty from York Holding sidings. Wagon No. 370368 was one of a batch of fifty-four built by Greenbrier during 2004 and has received unwanted graffiti markings.

HYA – 371102 – Dove Holes Quarry sidings – 7 June 2018
GBRf used a rake of the DB HTAs initially alongside its own HYA and IIA bogie coal hoppers on the various traffic flows. The original blue GBRf branding has already been removed leaving just the Coal lettering at the right-hand end. This wagon was built by IRS, Romania, between 2007/8 and converted by W.H. Davis to become a shortened length HYA wagon in the period between summer 2019 and spring 2020.

HYA – 371083 – Dove Holes Quarry sidings – 7 June 2018
This HYA has retained the original blue GBRf and Coal branding as shown. The HYA and IIA wagons still had the same issue as the HTAs in that the wagon was not being used to full capacity. GBRf and the wagon owners Nacco, Touax and VTG embarked on a similar conversion programme. A prototype HYA, No. 371051, was converted in early 2016. No. 371083 was also built by IRS, Romania, between 2007 and 2008 and converted by W.H. Davis between 2019 and 2020.

IIA – 37 70 6791 060-6 – Dove Holes Quarry sidings – 7 June 2018
A follow-on design of coal hoppers was constructed by IRS, Romania, in 2008 for Fastline Ltd as they captured a share of the UK railfreight coal market. Sadly, Fastline only lasted until March 2010, when parent company Jarvis ceased trading. The IIA wagons were originally leased from GE Rail Services and later passed into Touax ownership. Twenty-five IIAs were initially sent to W.H. Davis for conversion in late 2016 and gained revised numbers.

MJA – 502200 – Peak Forest – 7 June 2018
After the MJA 78.6 t twin-set wagons were delivered in 2003/4, Freightliner did not immediately order any additional wagons. However, two more wagons were built as single trial MJA wagons to a 77.2 t glw capacity. The first, was No. 502199 built by Greenbrier, 2005 fitted with ELH 'Opti-track' low-track force bogies. The second, seen here returning to Tunstead, was No. 502200, also built by Greenbrier, but in 2007 but fitted with Barber Easy Ride bogies.

HYA – 371045 – Dove Holes Quarry sidings – 9 August 2018
As wagons were converted by W.H. Davis for wagon lessor, NACCO at their Shirebrook workshops, some wagons were allocated to Dove Holes CEMEX traffic. Here we see the results of the conversion and the reduction from three down to two hopper discharge doors below the chassis solebar. The initial conversions did not gain a repaint and so looked rather tatty with a ghostly G very apparent on the bodysides, however the NACCO branding is newly applied.

JEA – BM 19706 – Peak Forest – 26 October 2018
The former Brunner Mond-owned JEA fleet of twenty-seven wagons was still owned by DB Cargo at the time of this photograph. The wagons had been reused during 2017 and early 2018 on a flow of glass cutlet between Tilbury Docks and the Encirc Glassworks at Ince in Cheshire. Their place on the Tunstead to Lostock limestone duties was covered by Freightliner Class 66s and their HIA hoppers, until DB resumed working the traffic in mid-2018.

JNA – 81 70 5500 497-9 – Stockport – 16 October 2019
As demands changed simple bogie box wagons were what the railfreight industry needed. The UIC coded Ealnos bogie box wagon became the design of choice. So far 860 wagons Ealnos wagons have been delivered to Ermewa, DB Cargo, VTG, GBRf and Touax. This wagon was from a batch of fifty built by Greenbrier-Astra Rail in Romania in 2017. Here, the single wagon is seen at Stockport station behind a GBRf Class 66 heading towards Crewe.

MWA – 81 70 5891 024-8 – Northwich – 28 May 2020
Freightliner also acquired their own version of the Ealnos wagons to a slightly different specification as can be seen in these next two photos. Also built by Greenbrier-Astra Rail in Romania in 2016, a batch of sixty-four wagons were outshopped in Freightliner's green company colours with side panels with the Freightliner branding on. Unfortunately, these wagons seem to soon attract the unauthorised attention of the graffiti community.

MWA – 81 70 5891 572-6 – Northwich – 28 May 2020
The second batch of MWAs were delivered in the new corporate grey and yellow colours of Genesse & Wyoming. They were the new owners of Freightliner. These new grey and yellow MWAs initially looked rather smart. But like the green MWAs soon suffered with graffiti. This rake of empty MWAs was returning from Bletchley to Barrow Hill sidings routed via Northwich and the Hope Valley for stabling pending the next duty from Tunstead quarry.

HHA – VTG – Peak Forest – 12 June 2020
VTG decided to embark on a similar conversion using surplus HHA bogie coal hoppers acquired in 2017 by NACCO/CIT and now owned by VTG and shortened to become aggregates hoppers. However, the donor HHAs had four hopper doors as opposed to the three on the HTAs and HYA/IIAs, and so needed more work to convert to two doors. Five wagons were on the rear of this Bredbury service – Nos 370303, 273, 277 and 398 are seen in this image.

HYA – 37 70 6791 061-4 – Dove Holes Quarry sidings – 5 October 2020
Following on from the initial HYA conversions for VTG and NACCO, subsequent wagons leaving W.H. Davis featured a repainted body side panel with new CEMEX, Touax and GB Railfreight branding as shown. On the body side you can see the staggered weld marks where the original wagons have been shortened to remove the middle discharge doors. This example shown is owned by Touax Rail Ltd.

HYA – 371015 – Dove Holes Quarry sidings – 5 October 2020

Further conversions to the same specifications were done for VTG Rail UK Ltd in 2019, when a batch of twelve wagons was converted for CEMEX traffic. On these HYAs the VTG logo was placed centrally on the wagon side as shown. This fleet of converted HYA wagons see widespread use on the major flows from Dove Holes with just a single set of unconverted HYAs still in use at the time of writing, these being used from Dove Holes and more recently Tunstead.

HYA – 371100 – Dove Holes Quarry sidings – 5 October 2020

A third and final variation in the livery omits the central logo of the owning company as this wagon is directly owned by GB Railfreight Limited. This time, the batch of nineteen HYAs converted did not have the VTG logo applied. The HTA/HYA/IIA conversion programme has been very successful in reusing redundant coal wagons and a similar conversion programme has since started with Freightliners HHA coal hoppers.

JPA – 81 70 9316 003-1 – Hope Earle's sidings – 5 October 2020
Hope Construction Materials placed an order for forty-eight new JPA tanks to the same design as the original Lafarge tanks. These VTG JPAs received numbers in the RIV range 81 70 9316 001–048 code Uacns built by Feldbinder in 2015/6. Further JPAs were also built for Hanson-HeidelbergCement Group (Nos 049–067) and a final three for Tarmac CRH (Nos 068–070). A further batch of twenty were built in 2016 for Colas Rail/Tarmac.

PCA – BCC 10795 – Hope Earle's sidings – 5 October 2020
By 2020, the PCA fleet was still soldering on in traffic from Hope. However, a start had been made to reduce the PCA size. For example, eleven Metalair-type PCAs were noted at the CF Booth scrapyard in Rotherham in early 2020. No. 10795 was still in traffic seen returning down to the rake in among a rake of thirty-four wagons that had recently returned from Dewsbury. Some PCAs are now in fly-ash traffic use bringing the material from Drax power station.

PCA – BCC 11017 – Hope Earle's sidings – 5 October 2020
Upon arrival at Earle's sidings, the Freightliner Class 66/6 reverses the rake into the Bottom End siding and splits the rake into two portions by using the loop line too. The Class 20 that is hired in from Harry Needle Railroad Company comes up the branch and often recombines the rake back into one single rake ready to amble along the 1½-mile-long branch to the works. No. 11017 brings up the rear of one such rake of PCAs now in their twilight years.

JNA – 81 70 5500 584-4 – Buxton Up Reception sidings – 7 October 2020
The second batch of JNA wagons delivered for GBRf was in association with wagon lessor Ermewa. Originally owned by French national railway operator SNCF, the Ermewa Group was sold off to write off a large proportion of SNCF's debt. Sale negotiations were still ongoing in 2021 at the time of writing. This wagon is on the tail-end of a rake of empties from Washwood Heath to Dowlow in the newly extended Up Reception sidings at Buxton.

HOA – 320042 – Peak Forest – 29 July 2021
One of the more colourful examples of graffiti applied to the sides of wagons has to be this one. This HOA wagon was in a rake with other DB-owned HOA and IIA hopper wagons forming a service from Peak Forest Up sidings to Dowlow Brigg's sidings, where the wagons would be loaded. This flow started during the 2020/1 pandemic and takes aggregates to Ely Papworth sidings twice a week at present.

HOA – 320019 – Peak Forest – 29 July 2021
The wagons for the Brigg's sidings to Ely service are stabled when not in service in the Up Holding sidings. From observations in July 2021, the wagons were split into two or three portions to fit into the sidings. Also, to take the empties to Dowlow, the rake was reformed and shunted into the Down and Up Through siding and the locomotive would run-round via Great Rocks Junction. This is one of the former CEMEX-liveried HOA wagons built in 2006.

IIA – 33 70 6955 077-8 – Peak Forest – 29 July 2021
Another of the former EWS Construction hopper wagons originally built for CEMEX traffic from Dove Holes quarry, this IIA wagon appears to have seen better days. The black staining down the wagon sides is a coating that was applied to a pool of HOA and IIA wagons for sand traffic. This ran from Middleton Towers near King's Lynn to the Encirc glassworks at Ince & Elton in Cheshire. Now back in aggregates traffic for DB Cargo from Dowlow to Ely.

HOA – 320054 – Peak Forest – 29 July 2021
A colourful addition to the base DB Schenker red livery adorns the side of this HOA. The HOAs for EWS were later followed by a separate order for wagon lessor Ermewa and branded for Tarmac traffic then VTG for Mendip Rail both branded accordingly. These wagons were built by Astra Rail during 2015/6. Confusingly, a third batch of HOAs exist operated by lessor Touax, but the actual design is more like the EWS Construction-owned IIA wagons.

MWA – 81 70 5891 007-3 – Buxton Up Reception sidings – 29 July 2021
Up until 2020, Hindlow quarry was purely a processing quarry for incoming trainloads of limestone moved the short distance from Tunstead. Apart from the quicklime traffic in the CSA tanks described above, there was no outbound traffic. Tarmac Buxton Lime & Cement decided to resume quarrying to supply stone High-Speed Rail HS2 project. This MWA is on the end of a rake parked in the Buxton Up Reception sidings going to Small Heath (Birmingham).

IIA – 37 70 6791 000-2 – Peak Forest – 29 July 2021
GBRf operate most of their hopper services using the converted shortened HYA hoppers but have several sets of the original HYA/IIA coal hoppers in traffic too for aggregates. One set worked alongside the converted wagons from Dove Holes from 2018 to 2020. Another Touax rake has since appeared this time working from Tunstead quarry to Washwood Heath, which is thought to be another HS2-related flow – one of six currently active to the Midlands area.

JNA – 81 70 5500 691-7 – Peak Forest – 8 August 2021
This smart, clean-looking aquamarine blue-liveried JNA box wagon is part of a rake of twenty-four that has just arrived at Peak Forest from Chaddesden sidings, Derby, behind Class 60 No. 60028. This service operates on behalf of DB Cargo and uses DCRail Class 60s to move the stone to Brandon Down sidings via an overnight stop at Chaddesden sidings. A batch of fifteen Ealnos-type JNAs were delivered for VTG in 2019, followed by a further thirty-five in 2020.

JNAs – 81 70 5500 776-7 – Northwich – 17 September 2021
A batch of fifty JNA Ealnos box wagons were ordered by VTG and delivered in 2019 for general spot hire traffics. The next fifty wagons are numbered 81 70 5500 754–803 and wear a plain silver livery with the VTG logo and lettering on the second and third bodyside panels as shown. GBRf hired in additional silver VTG JNAs to work alongside its own fleet of JNAs. This train is from Ham Hall to Hindlow and is one of several active Midlands HS2 aggregates flows.